W9-BIH-235

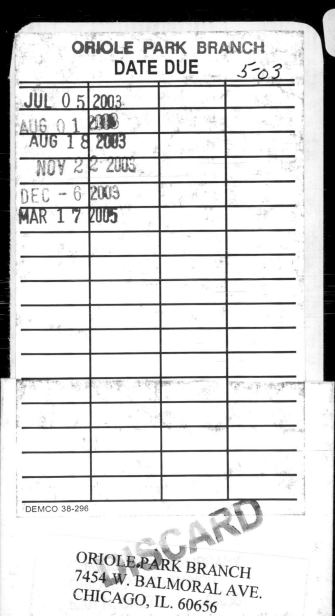

I didn't know that some planes hover

© Aladdin Books Ltd 1998
© U.S. text 1998
Produced by
Aladdin Books Ltd
28 Percy Street
London W1P 0LD

First published in the United States in 1998 by
Copper Beech Books,
an imprint of
The Millbrook Press
2 Old New Milford Road
Brookfield, Connecticut 06804

Concept, editorial, and design by
David West Children's Books

Illustrators: Ross Watton and Jo Moore

Printed in Belgium

Library of Congress Cataloging-in-Publication Data
Petty, Kate.
Some planes hover and other amazing facts about flying machines / by
Kate Petty ; illustrated by Ross Watton and Jo Moore.
p. cm. — (I didn't know that—)
Includes index.
Summary: Presents information about a variety of flying machines, from
the earliest balloon and airplanes to jets, rocket-powered craft, and
planes of the future.
ISBN 0-7613-0713-3 (lib. bdg.). — ISBN 0-7613-0645-5 (trade)
1. Flying machines—Juvenile literature.
[1. Flying machines. 2. Aeronautics.]
I. Watton, Ross, ill. II. Moore, Jo, ill. III. Title. IV. Series.
TL547.P424 1998   97-31923
629.133—dc21   CIP AC
5 4 3 2 1

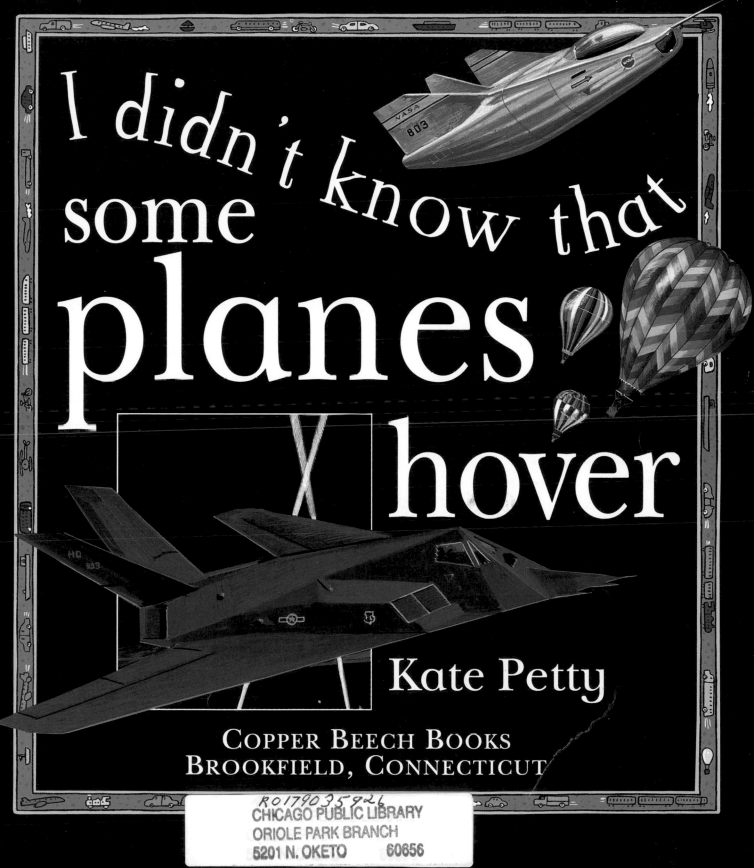

I didn't know that
some
planes
hover

Kate Petty

COPPER BEECH BOOKS
BROOKFIELD, CONNECTICUT

I didn't know that

Introduction

Did *you* know that one plane had 200 wings? ... that some planes have none? ... that helicopters can fly upside down when they loop the loop?

Discover for yourself amazing facts about flying machines, from the earliest hot-air balloons to the latest computer-controlled machines that can change shape as they fly.

 Watch for this symbol that means there is a fun project for you to try.

Is it true or is it false? Watch for this symbol and try to answer the question before reading on for the answer.

Don't forget to check the borders for extra amazing facts.

I didn't know that

you can fly with hot air. As air heats up, it expands and so becomes lighter than the air around it. If you fill a balloon with hot air it will rise up. Gas burners heated the air in this balloon.

The Montgolfier brothers made this famous balloon from linen and paper. The air inside was heated by burning straw. It carried two men across Paris on the first-ever manned flight in November 1783.

Balloon pilots depend on the wind for speed and direction. This makes any balloon travel uncertain. However, in 1987 Richard Branson and Per Lindstrand managed to fly in a balloon all the way across the Atlantic Ocean.

SEARCH & FIND Can you find the shaped balloon? FIND & SEARCH

In 1997 Steve Fosset set the long-distance record of 10,356 miles.

I didn't know that

airships contain no air – well, not air as we know it. Some gases are lighter than air even without being heated. The first airships were filled with hydrogen gas. They were powered by engines and could be steered.

The *Hindenburg* burst into flames in 1937. During World War II, hydrogen-filled barrage balloons were tethered over London. Enemy planes caught fire when they flew into them or into the cables that tethered them.

The first airship, flown by Henri Giffard in 1852, was steam-powered.

Modern airships are filled with helium gas. Helium gas is lighter than air but it won't catch fire. This airship (right) can carry 20 passengers. It uses swiveling *propellers* to help it steer, take off, and land.

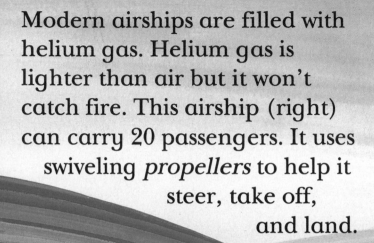

Hindenburg

Compare a helium-filled balloon with an ordinary one filled with air. Which one floats up on its own? Make sure you don't let go!

 True or false?

The Space Shuttle is a *glider*.

Answer: **True**

When the Space Shuttle reenters the Earth's atmosphere on its way home, it glides halfway around the world before it comes in to land.

Glider

Many of the first "heavier-than-air" flying machines that were tested in the early 1900s were gliders. The Wright brothers experimented with gliders for four years before their first powered flight in 1903.

In 1849, a triplane glider lifted a ten-year-old boy into the air.

I didn't know that

some planes fly without engines.
Once a glider has been towed into the
air it uses rising currents of hot air
(thermals) to gain height. The
curved shape of the wings keeps the
glider airborne as it moves forward.

SEARCH & FIND

Can you find the gliding seagull?

FIND & SEARCH

The German aviator Otto
Lilienthal (right) made well
over 2,000 glides before
crashing to his death in
1896. His gliders were
very similar to modern
hang gliders.

Hang glider

I didn't know that

some planes had three wings. *Biplanes* and triplanes get strength and *lift* from their wings. This can make them more tough and maneuverable than monoplanes.

The *Phillips Multiplane* of 1907 had 200 narrow, slatlike wings. Its designer, Horatio Phillips, gave it up after a few disappointing tests.

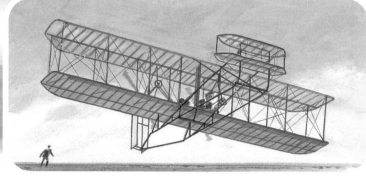

The Wright brothers' first powered flight in 1903 was in a biplane. They had spent many months making an engine that would be light enough.

SEARCH & FIND & SEARCH & FIND &

Can you find the *Bleriot* monoplane?

Fokker DRI

Vickers-Vimy Biplane

True or false?

A biplane was the first plane to cross the Atlantic Ocean.

Answer: **True**

It was a *Vickers-Vimy Biplane* flown by British pilots Alcock and Brown in 1919.

Lindbergh crossed the Atlantic solo from New York to Paris in 1927.

I didn't know that

planes can land on water.

Early seaplanes used the sea as a runway. One crossed the Atlantic in 1919, refueling on the water. Passengers could fly long distances in the 1930s in flying boats like this *Boeing 314*.

The German *Junkers F13* that appeared in 1919 could be fitted with floats, wheels, or even skis. It was used to open up routes in remote areas of Russia and China.

The first airmail services started in Australia in 1914 and in the U.S. in 1918. Flying boats were later used to increase the overseas service.

Boeing 314

The wooden *Spruce Goose* was the largest seaplane ever. It only flew once.

The latest flying boat is the *Sea Wing* (right), made in Tasmania. It is actually a boat, but it takes off from the water and flies above the water at a speed of 160 knots. It is especially good at flying in rough, stormy weather.

True or false?
The first seaplane flew in 1910.

Answer: **True**
Henri Fabre took off from a lake in the seaplane *Canard*. He flew for one mile, just 13 feet above the water.

AMERICAN AIRWAYS SYSTEM

NC 18604

I didn't know that

a *Comet* was the first *jet* airliner. In 1952, passengers were thrilled by their fast, comfortable flight from England to South Africa in the new British-designed jet. Later, the *Boeing 707* became more popular as a commercial airliner.

SEARCH & FIND
Can you find the pilot?
FIND & SEARCH

The first encounter between high-speed, jet-powered craft took place in 1944 when a British *Gloster Meteor* intercepted a pilotless *Doodlebug* (German V1 flying bomb) over London.

Comet

G-ALZK

COMET

The smallest jet plane, the *Silver Bullet*, weighs about as much as three people.

True or false?

You can't travel faster than the speed of sound.

Answer: **False**

Concorde (above right) first flew faster than the speed of sound (*Mach 1*) in 1969. In 1997, the British *Thrust* car became the first to reach *supersonic* speeds on land.

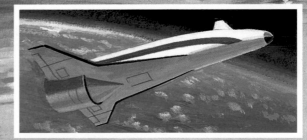

Future flight will be faster in space where there is no air friction. Planes will need *ramjets* to hop above the *atmosphere*.

X-24A

True or false?

Planes have to have wings to fly.

Answer: **False**

This *X-24A* was used for NASA research into a plane that got its lift from the shape of the whole body and not just the wing. In 1970, it flew at 781 mph (Mach 1.19).

I didn't know that

some planes are rocket-powered. Liquid-fueled rocket engines power the fastest planes. The *X-15*s were experimental aircraft. In 1967, the *X-15 A-2* reached 4,507 mph (Mach 6.86).

Chuck Yeager was the first pilot ever to go supersonic. In 1947, he flew in a *Bell X-1* at 670 mph (Mach 1.015).

Can you find the bomber that launched X-15?
SEARCH & FIND & SEARCH & FIND &

Some very fast cars use rocket power too. In 1970 *The Blue Flame* (below) managed a record speed of 626 mph. This is still the record for a rocket car.

X-15 Rocket plane

Burning rocket fuel produces hot gases that expand and escape downward, thrusting the rocket upward. See how this works by blowing up a balloon and watching it shoot forward as the air escapes.

I didn't know that

planes can change shape.

Some modern planes, like the *Panavia Tornado*, can change shape in midair. Others have a variety of wing designs, with wings fixed in different shapes and positions.

Lockheed F-117 Stealth fighter

True or false?
Planes can be invisible.

Answer: **True**
The unusual-looking *Lockheed F-117 Stealth* fighters are designed to absorb or deflect *radar* signals, which means that they don't show up on radar screens.

The *Flying Wing*, built in 1950, was just that, shaped like an enormous wing.

Panavia Tornado with wings swept back.

Some new aircraft look back-to-front! The wings on this NASA *X-29* (above) face forward to help the plane turn tight corners at high speed.

Panavia Tornado with wings extended outward.

The fastest jet-powered aircraft was the *Lockheed SR-71* (right), a spy plane called *Blackbird*. It flies at high speeds and altitudes to avoid detection.

The autogiro can't hover. Its main *rotor* has no engine to power it. The engine only powers the propeller which drives the autogiro forward. The rotor then rotates in the wind and produces lift.

Apache AH-64

Look for natural helicopters! Some tree seeds are dispersed with "rotors." Watch sycamore or ash seeds as they spin away from the tree on the wind.

I didn't know that

helicopters can fly upside down – when they loop the loop! And they can fly backward and sideways too. The rotor blades have an *airfoil* shape that creates lift as they rotate.

Helicopters can move vertically and hover, so they're very useful for rescuing people from a tight spot – such as a busy town, a mountain peak, or a stormy sea.

I didn't know that

some planes hover. This *Harrier GR5* bomber does! It's a VTOL aircraft, which stands for Vertical Take-Off and Landing. Nozzles direct the engine power downward for taking off and hovering, or backward for flying forward.

This *Osprey* is a strange bird – a cross between a plane and a helicopter! The rotors are upright for vertical takeoff and then tilt forward for normal flight.

Planes that can take off and land at a steep angle are useful in built-up city areas. This little *DASH-7* is landing at a busy city airport. It is a STOL plane – Short Take-Off and Landing.

Harrier jump-jet

Now humans can hover with a flying belt! A jet of superheated air rushes downward from a jet-pack, thrusting the person off the ground – but only for 28 seconds!

True or false?
People walk on wings.

Answer: **True**
In the 1920s and 30s "wing walkers" were strapped to the wing of a low-flying plane to advertise a product or a movie.

Skilled pilots can perform some amazing stunts. It looks scary when they stall (stop) and then restart the engines, but they know what they're doing!

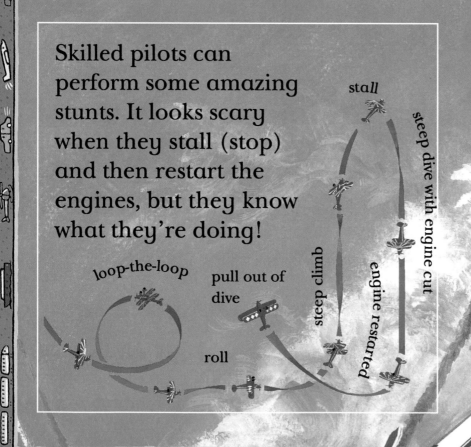

stall

steep dive with engine cut

steep climb

engine restarted

loop-the-loop

pull out of dive

roll

F-16 Fighting Falcon
U.S. display team

A *YF-22* fighter plane can literally "fly on its tail" just by altering the direction of the *thrust*.

I didn't know that

planes can fly by wire. In today's aircraft, computers relay the pilot's instructions along electric wires to motors that move the *ailerons*, *elevators*, and *rudder*. Older planes used cables connected to the pilot's controls.

27

I didn't know that

planes could be pedal-powered. The *Gossamer Albatross* was pedaled across the English Channel in 1979. It weighed as much as a small child! The pedals turned the propeller.

In the Greek myth, Daedalus and Icarus flew out of captivity using wings of feathers and wax. But Icarus flew too close to the sun – and his wings melted!

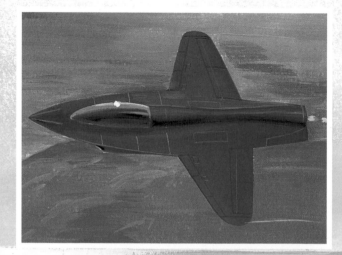

Future fighter planes will have "active aeroelastic wings," computerized to twist and change shape according to flight conditions. The planes will look very distinctive – they won't need any *tailplanes*!

Back in the 1480s, Leonardo da Vinci sketched designs for man-powered flight.

Voyager is an unusual light aircraft that flew non-stop around the world in 1986 on a single tank of fuel. The two pilots spent the nine-day journey in a pod that was only 23 inches wide. Ouch!

Gossamer Albatross

Glossary

Ailerons, elevators, and rudder
Movable panels on wings, tailplane, and tail for tilting and turning the plane.

Airfoil
Wing shape best suited to giving lift. The airflow is faster over the curved upper surface so air pressure above is lower than air pressure below.

Airship
Boat-shaped, gas-filled balloon that is power-driven and steerable.

Atmosphere
Air surrounding the Earth.

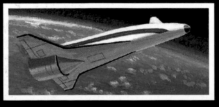

Biplane
Plane with two sets of wings, one above the other.

Glider
Aircraft without engines that relies on air currents to stay in the air.

Jet
In a jet engine, air is sucked in, mixed with fuel, ignited, and forced out in a jet that moves the aircraft forward.

Lift
Force that keeps an airplane up, created when the air pressure below is higher than the air pressure above the wing or craft.

Mach 1

The speed of sound, named after physicist Ernst Mach. Mach 2 is twice the speed of sound.

Mercury

A seaplane that was lifted into the air by a bigger aircraft so saving fuel. It then set a seaplane straight-line distance record of 5,961 miles.

Propellers

Blades that rotate in air or water to move a plane or a boat along.

Radar

Stands for RAdio Detection And Ranging, used for detecting objects by bouncing radio waves off them.

Ramjet

Type of engine that can provide extra power only when the aircraft is moving.

Rotor

Rotating blade that breaks up airflow to give lift.

Supersonic

Faster than the speed of sound. A supersonic aircraft breaking the sound barrier makes a "sonic boom" as shock waves reach the ground.

Tailplane

A small horizontal wing at the tail end of an aircraft.

Thrust

The force that pushes an aircraft forward.

Ind**ex**